The Build Journal

Tuner Press
a division of Storyopolis Ventures LLC
66 West Flagler St, Ste 900-3272
Miami, FL 33130
www.tunerpress.com
www.tunercartoons.com

Who This Journal Is For

This journal was built for owners who take their vehicles seriously.

It's for the builder who stays late in the garage.

The driver who knows every sound the car makes.

The owner who understands that pride isn't loud — it's documented.

Whether you own:

- A classic
- A restomod
- A track car
- A show build
- A weekend cruiser
- Or a small collection

If you've invested time, money, and thought into your vehicle, this journal belongs with it.

This isn't a generic maintenance notebook.

It's a structured record of your build, your investment, and your stewardship.

Problems This Journal Solves

Disorganized Records

Receipts in boxes. Notes in your phone. Photos scattered across folders.
This journal brings everything into one organized, durable record.

Forgotten Details

You remember upgrading the suspension — but which brand?
You swapped the cam — but what specs?
You researched tires –- but will your son know what you looked at
Years from now, those details matter.

Untracked Investment

Most owners underestimate what they have into their vehicle.
Parts add up. Labor adds up.
This journal tracks cumulative totals clearly and honestly.

Insurance & Resale Confidence

A documented vehicle stands apart.
Clear records support insured value and justify asking price.
Buyers trust documentation.

Build Story

Every vehicle has a timeline.
This journal captures not only what was done — but why.
It turns memory into record.
And record into legacy.

HOW TO USE YOUR JOURNAL

This journal is designed to work in the real world — on a workbench, in a shop, or on your kitchen table.

You do not need to fill it out perfectly.

You need to fill it out consistently.

1. Start With the Vehicle Profile

Complete the overview section first:
- Year / Make / Model
- VIN
- Engine / transmission specs
- Current mileage
- Purchase details

This sets your starting point.

If the vehicle has prior history, summarize what you know. You can always expand later.

2. Log Every Change

Each Modification Entry page is for:
- Parts installations
- Repairs
- Custom fabrication
- Performance upgrades
- Major service

Record:
- Date
- Mileage
- Part name and brand
- Cost
- Labor (paid or self-performed)
- Notes or reasoning

If you performed the work yourself, you may record estimated labor value. Your time matters.

3. Track Maintenance

Routine maintenance protects your investment.

Use the maintenance logs to record:
- Oil changes
- Brake service
- Fluid changes
- Belt and filter replacement
- Alignments
- Tire service

Consistency builds reliability — and credibility.

4. Update the Investment Summary

The Investment Summary pages provide clarity.

Periodically total:
- Parts
- Labor
- Category spending
- Running cumulative investment

This gives you:
- A clear financial picture
- A defensible declared value
- Real leverage during resale

Most owners are surprised by the true number.

5. Document Milestones

Use the milestone pages for moments that matter:
- First startup
- Dyno results
- Track times
- Awards
- Show appearances
- Major rebuild completions

Cars evolve. This journal captures that evolution.

CONTENTS

VEHICLE MASTER RECORD

Asset ID: _________

Owner: _________

VEHICLE OVERVIEW

Year: _________________________________

Make: _________________________________

Model: ________________________________

VIN: __________________________________

Factory Color: ________________________

License Plate #: ______________________

Purchase Date: ________________________

Purchase Price: _______________________

Title (clean/rebuilt/salvage): _________

BUILD OBJECTIVE

- ☐ Show Vehicle
- ☐ Race Vehicle
- ☐ Restoration
- ☐ Restomod
- ☐ Street Cruiser
- ☐ Daily Driver
- ☐ Custom Build
- ☐ Commercial Vehicle
- ☐ Other_____________

PRIMARY GOAL

____

____

____

____

CURRENT SPECIFICATIONS

ENGINE

Engine Type: __________________________

Displacement: _________________________

Builder: ______________________________

Install Date: _________________________

TRANSMISSION

Type: _________________________________

Builder: ______________________________

Gear Ratio: ___________________________

REAR END

Differential Type:_____________________

Gear Ratio: ___________________________

SUSPENSION

Type (coilover/leaf/air):______________

Brand: ________________________________

BRAKES

Brand/configruation): _________________

PAINT

Color: ________________________________

Paint Code:____________________________

WHEELS

Brand/Model:___________________________

TIRES

Brand/Model:___________________________

INTERIOR

Color: ________________________________

Fabric_________________________________

Seats _________________________________

CONDITION & REPAIR HISTORY

Asset ID: _________

Owner: _________

Date	Mileage	Issue/ Damage	Repair Performed	Shop	Notes

FACTORY DOCUMENTATION

Production Date:_______________________

Assembly Plant: _______________________

Build Sheet/Build Sheet Photo (attach below):

MASTER PARTS INVENTORY & SOURCING LOG

Asset ID: ____________

Owner: ____________

Part ID	Category	Brand	Supplier	Install Date	Cost

MASTER PARTS INVENTORY & SOURCING LOG

Asset ID: __________
Owner: __________

Part ID	Category	Brand	Supplier	Install Date	Cost

MASTER PARTS INVENTORY & SOURCING LOG

Asset ID: ________
Owner: ________

Part ID	Category	Brand	Supplier	Install Date	Cost

MASTER PARTS INVENTORY & SOURCING LOG

Asset ID: ___________

Owner: ___________

Part ID	Category	Brand	Supplier	Install Date	Cost

MODIFICATION ENTRY

Asset ID:_________

Owner: _________

ENTRY #:

Install Date: _______________________________

 Mileage at Install: _________________________

PART INFORMATION

Part Name: _______________________________

Model #: _________________________________

Brand : __________________________________

Supplier: _________________________________

Website: _________________________________

Order #: _________________________________

COST BREAKDOWN

Parts Cost: $_______________________________

Shipping: $ _______________________________

Tax: $____________________________________

Labor: $ _________________________________

TOTAL INSTALL COST: $ _____________________

Total Build Costs to Date: $ ________________

CATEGORY

- ☐ Engine
- ☐ Suspension
- ☐ Transmission
- ☐ Interior
- ☐ Exterior
- ☐ Wheels & Tires
- ☐ Electrical
- ☐ Exhaust
- ☐ Other_________

INSTALL DETAILS

Installed by: _______________________________

Install time: (hrs)__________________________

Tools used: _______________________________

____

Torque Specs/Key Notes: ____________________

____

RESULTS:

Performance Change: _______________________

Further Adjustments:________________________

MODIFICATION ENTRY

ENTRY #:

Install Date: ______________________________

 Mileage at Install: ______________________

PART INFORMATION

Part Name: ______________________________

Model #: ________________________________

Brand : _________________________________

Supplier: ________________________________

Website: ________________________________

Order #: _________________________________

COST BREAKDOWN

Parts Cost: $ ____________________________

Shipping: $ ______________________________

Tax: $ ___________________________________

Labor: $ _________________________________

TOTAL INSTALL COST: $ __________________

Total Build Costs to Date: $ _____________

CATEGORY

☐ Engine

☐ Suspension

☐ Transmission

☐ Interior

☐ Exterior

☐ Wheels & Tires

☐ Electrical

☐ Exhaust

☐ Other__________

INSTALL DETAILS

Installed by: ____________________________

Install time: (hrs) _______________________

Tools used: ______________________________

____

Torque Specs/Key Notes: _________________

____

RESULTS:

Performance Change: ____________________

Further Adjustments: ____________________

MODIFICATION ENTRY

Asset ID: _________

Owner: _________

ENTRY #:

Install Date: _______________________

 Mileage at Install: ___________________

PART INFORMATION

Part Name: _______________________

Model #: _______________________

Brand : _______________________

Supplier: _______________________

Website: _______________________

Order #: _______________________

COST BREAKDOWN

Parts Cost: $ _______________________

Shipping: $ _______________________

Tax: $ _______________________

Labor: $ _______________________

TOTAL INSTALL COST: $ _______________

Total Build Costs to Date: $ _____________

CATEGORY

- ☐ Engine
- ☐ Suspension
- ☐ Transmission
- ☐ Interior
- ☐ Exterior
- ☐ Wheels & Tires
- ☐ Electrical
- ☐ Exhaust
- ☐ Other_________

INSTALL DETAILS

Installed by: _______________________

Install time: (hrs)_______________________

Tools used: _______________________

____

Torque Specs/Key Notes:_______________________

____

RESULTS:

Performance Change: _______________________

Further Adjustments:_______________________

MODIFICATION ENTRY

Asset ID: _________

Owner: _________

ENTRY #:

Install Date: _______________________________

Mileage at Install: ____________________

PART INFORMATION

Part Name: _______________________

Model #: _________________________

Brand : __________________________

Supplier: ________________________

Website: _________________________

Order #: _________________________

COST BREAKDOWN

Parts Cost: $______________________________

Shipping: $_______________________________

Tax: $____________________________________

Labor: $__________________________________

TOTAL INSTALL COST: $____________________

Total Build Costs to Date: $______________

CATEGORY

- ☐ Engine
- ☐ Suspension
- ☐ Transmission
- ☐ Interior
- ☐ Exterior
- ☐ Wheels & Tires
- ☐ Electrical
- ☐ Exhaust
- ☐ Other_________

INSTALL DETAILS

Installed by: ______________________

Install time: (hrs)__________________

Tools used: ____

____

Torque Specs/Key Notes:______________________________________

____

RESULTS:

Performance Change: ____

Further Adjustments:____

MODIFICATION ENTRY

Asset ID: _________

Owner: _________

ENTRY #:

Install Date: _______________________

 Mileage at Install: _________________

PART INFORMATION

Part Name: _____________________

Model #: _______________________

Brand : ________________________

Supplier: ______________________

Website: _______________________

Order #: _______________________

COST BREAKDOWN

Parts Cost: $_____________________

Shipping: $______________________

Tax: $__________________________

Labor: $________________________

TOTAL INSTALL COST: $_____________

Total Build Costs to Date: $_________

CATEGORY

- [ ] Engine
- [ ] Suspension
- [ ] Transmission
- [ ] Interior
- [ ] Exterior
- [ ] Wheels & Tires
- [ ] Electrical
- [ ] Exhaust
- [ ] Other_________

INSTALL DETAILS

Installed by: ____________________

Install time: (hrs)_______________

Tools used: _____________________

____

Torque Specs/Key Notes: __________

____

RESULTS:

Performance Change: _____________

Further Adjustments:______________

MODIFICATION ENTRY

Asset ID: _________
Owner: _________

ENTRY #:

Install Date: _______________________________

 Mileage at Install: ____________________________

PART INFORMATION

Part Name: _________________________________

Model #: ___________________________________

Brand : ____________________________________

Supplier: ___________________________________

Website: ___________________________________

Order #: ___________________________________

COST BREAKDOWN

Parts Cost: $ _______________________________

Shipping: $ _________________________________

Tax: $ _____________________________________

Labor: $ ___________________________________

TOTAL INSTALL COST: $ ______________________

Total Build Costs to Date: $ ________________

CATEGORY

- ☐ Engine
- ☐ Suspension
- ☐ Transmission
- ☐ Interior
- ☐ Exterior
- ☐ Wheels & Tires
- ☐ Electrical
- ☐ Exhaust
- ☐ Other_________

INSTALL DETAILS

Installed by: _______________________________

Install time: (hrs)__________________________

Tools used: ________________________________

____

Torque Specs/Key Notes:_____________________________

____

RESULTS:

Performance Change: _______________________________

Further Adjustments:________________________________

MODIFICATION ENTRY

Asset ID: _________
Owner: _________

ENTRY #:

Install Date: _______________________

 Mileage at Install: _________________

PART INFORMATION

Part Name: _______________________

Model #: _______________________

Brand : _______________________

Supplier: _______________________

Website: _______________________

Order #: _______________________

COST BREAKDOWN

Parts Cost: $ _______________________

Shipping: $ _______________________

Tax: $ _______________________

Labor: $ _______________________

TOTAL INSTALL COST: $ _______________

Total Build Costs to Date: $ ___________

CATEGORY

☐ Engine

☐ Suspension

☐ Transmission

☐ Interior

☐ Exterior

☐ Wheels & Tires

☐ Electrical

☐ Exhaust

☐ Other_________

INSTALL DETAILS

Installed by: _______________________

Install time: (hrs)_______________________

Tools used: _______________________

____

Torque Specs/Key Notes:_______________________

____

RESULTS:

Performance Change: _______________________

Further Adjustments:_______________________

MODIFICATION ENTRY

Asset ID: _________
Owner: _________

ENTRY #:

Install Date: _______________________

 Mileage at Install: _________________

PART INFORMATION

Part Name: _____________________

Model #: ______________________

Brand : _______________________

Supplier: ______________________

Website: ______________________

Order #: ______________________

COST BREAKDOWN

Parts Cost: $ __________________________

Shipping: $ ___________________________

Tax: $ _______________________________

Labor: $ _____________________________

TOTAL INSTALL COST: $ _______________

Total Build Costs to Date: $ ____________

CATEGORY

- ☐ Engine
- ☐ Suspension
- ☐ Transmission
- ☐ Interior
- ☐ Exterior
- ☐ Wheels & Tires
- ☐ Electrical
- ☐ Exhaust
- ☐ Other_________

INSTALL DETAILS

Installed by: ___________________________

Install time: (hrs)______________________

Tools used: ____

____

Torque Specs/Key Notes:________________________________

____

RESULTS:

Performance Change: ___________________________________

Further Adjustments:____________________________________

MODIFICATION ENTRY

Asset ID: __________
Owner: __________

ENTRY #:

Install Date: _______________________________

 Mileage at Install: __________________________

PART INFORMATION

Part Name: _______________________________

Model #: _________________________________

Brand : __________________________________

Supplier: ________________________________

Website: _________________________________

Order #: _________________________________

COST BREAKDOWN

Parts Cost: $ _____________________________

Shipping: $ _______________________________

Tax: $ ____________________________________

Labor: $ __________________________________

TOTAL INSTALL COST: $ _____________________

Total Build Costs to Date: $ ______________

CATEGORY

- ☐ Engine
- ☐ Suspension
- ☐ Transmission
- ☐ Interior
- ☐ Exterior
- ☐ Wheels & Tires
- ☐ Electrical
- ☐ Exhaust
- ☐ Other________

INSTALL DETAILS

Installed by: _____________________________

Install time: (hrs)_______________________

Tools used: _______________________________

____

Torque Specs/Key Notes:___________________

____

RESULTS:

Performance Change: ______________________

Further Adjustments:______________________

MODIFICATION ENTRY

Asset ID: ________

Owner: ________

ENTRY #:

Install Date: __________________________

Mileage at Install: ___________________

PART INFORMATION

Part Name: _________________________

Model #: ___________________________

Brand : ____________________________

Supplier: __________________________

Website: ___________________________

Order #: ___________________________

COST BREAKDOWN

Parts Cost: \$_________________________

Shipping: \$_________________________

Tax: \$____________________________

Labor: \$___________________________

TOTAL INSTALL COST: \$________________

Total Build Costs to Date: \$_____________

CATEGORY

- ☐ Engine
- ☐ Suspension
- ☐ Transmission
- ☐ Interior
- ☐ Exterior
- ☐ Wheels & Tires
- ☐ Electrical
- ☐ Exhaust
- ☐ Other________

INSTALL DETAILS

Installed by: _______________________

Install time: (hrs) ___________________

Tools used: ____

Torque Specs/Key Notes: ____

RESULTS:

Performance Change: ____

Further Adjustments: ____

MODIFICATION ENTRY

ENTRY #:

Install Date: _______________________________

Mileage at Install: _______________________

PART INFORMATION

Part Name: _________________________________

Model #: ___________________________________

Brand : ____________________________________

Supplier: __________________________________

Website: ___________________________________

Order #: ___________________________________

COST BREAKDOWN

Parts Cost: $ _______________________________

Shipping: $ _________________________________

Tax: $ ______________________________________

Labor: $ ____________________________________

TOTAL INSTALL COST: $ ______________________

Total Build Costs to Date: $ _______________

CATEGORY

☐ Engine

☐ Suspension

☐ Transmission

☐ Interior

☐ Exterior

☐ Wheels & Tires

☐ Electrical

☐ Exhaust

☐ Other__________

INSTALL DETAILS

Installed by: _______________________________

Install time: (hrs)_________________________

Tools used: ________________________________

____

Torque Specs/Key Notes:_____________________

____

RESULTS:

Performance Change: _______________________

Further Adjustments:________________________

MODIFICATION ENTRY

Asset ID: _________
Owner: _________

ENTRY #:

Install Date: _______________________

 Mileage at Install: _______________

PART INFORMATION

Part Name: _____________________

Model #: _______________________

Brand : ________________________

Supplier: _______________________

Website: _______________________

Order #: ________________________

COST BREAKDOWN

Parts Cost: $_____________________

Shipping: $ _____________________

Tax: $___________________________

Labor: $ ________________________

TOTAL INSTALL COST: $ ___________

Total Build Costs to Date: $ __________

CATEGORY

- [ ] Engine
- [ ] Suspension
- [ ] Transmission
- [ ] Interior
- [ ] Exterior
- [ ] Wheels & Tires
- [ ] Electrical
- [ ] Exhaust
- [ ] Other_________

INSTALL DETAILS

Installed by: ____________________

Install time: (hrs)_______________

Tools used: ______________________

____

Torque Specs/Key Notes:___________

____

RESULTS:

Performance Change: _____________

Further Adjustments:______________

MODIFICATION ENTRY

Asset ID: _________

Owner: _________

ENTRY #:

Install Date: _______________________

 Mileage at Install: _______________

PART INFORMATION

Part Name: _______________________

Model #: _________________________

Brand : __________________________

Supplier: ________________________

Website: _________________________

Order #: _________________________

COST BREAKDOWN

Parts Cost: $ _____________________

Shipping: $ _______________________

Tax: $ ___________________________

Labor: $ _________________________

TOTAL INSTALL COST: $ _____________

Total Build Costs to Date: $ __________

CATEGORY

- ☐ Engine
- ☐ Suspension
- ☐ Transmission
- ☐ Interior
- ☐ Exterior
- ☐ Wheels & Tires
- ☐ Electrical
- ☐ Exhaust
- ☐ Other_________

INSTALL DETAILS

Installed by: ______________________

Install time: (hrs)_________________

Tools used: ____

____

Torque Specs/Key Notes: _____________________________________

____

RESULTS:

Performance Change: ____

Further Adjustments:____

MODIFICATION ENTRY

Asset ID: _________
Owner: _________

ENTRY #:

Install Date: _______________________________

 Mileage at Install: _____________________

PART INFORMATION

Part Name: _________________________________

Model #: ___________________________________

Brand : ____________________________________

Supplier: __________________________________

Website: ___________________________________

Order #: ___________________________________

COST BREAKDOWN

Parts Cost: $ ______________________________

Shipping: $ ________________________________

Tax: $ _____________________________________

Labor: $ ___________________________________

TOTAL INSTALL COST: $ ______________________

Total Build Costs to Date: $ _______________

CATEGORY

☐ Engine
☐ Suspension
☐ Transmission
☐ Interior
☐ Exterior
☐ Wheels & Tires
☐ Electrical
☐ Exhaust
☐ Other_________

INSTALL DETAILS

Installed by: ______________________________

Install time: (hrs)_________________________

Tools used: ________________________________

____

Torque Specs/Key Notes:_____________________

____

RESULTS:

Performance Change: ________________________

Further Adjustments:________________________

MODIFICATION ENTRY

Asset ID: _________

Owner: _________

ENTRY #:

Install Date: _______________________

 Mileage at Install: ________________

PART INFORMATION

Part Name: ____________________________

Model #: _____________________________

Brand : ______________________________

Supplier: _____________________________

Website: _____________________________

Order #: _____________________________

COST BREAKDOWN

Parts Cost: $ ________________________

Shipping: $ _________________________

Tax: $ ______________________________

Labor: $ ____________________________

TOTAL INSTALL COST: $ _______________

Total Build Costs to Date: $ ____________

CATEGORY

- ☐ Engine
- ☐ Suspension
- ☐ Transmission
- ☐ Interior
- ☐ Exterior
- ☐ Wheels & Tires
- ☐ Electrical
- ☐ Exhaust
- ☐ Other_________

INSTALL DETAILS

Installed by: ___________________________

Install time: (hrs)_____________________

Tools used: ____

____

Torque Specs/Key Notes:____

____

RESULTS:

Performance Change: ____

Further Adjustments:____

MODIFICATION ENTRY

Asset ID: _________
Owner: __________

ENTRY #:

Install Date: _______________________________

 Mileage at Install: ____________________________

PART INFORMATION

Part Name: _________________________________

Model #: ___________________________________

Brand : ____________________________________

Supplier: ___________________________________

Website: ___________________________________

Order #: ___________________________________

COST BREAKDOWN

Parts Cost: $_________________________________

Shipping: $ _________________________________

Tax: $_____________________________________

Labor: $ ___________________________________

TOTAL INSTALL COST: $ ____________________

Total Build Costs to Date: $ _______________

CATEGORY

- ☐ Engine
- ☐ Suspension
- ☐ Transmission
- ☐ Interior
- ☐ Exterior
- ☐ Wheels & Tires
- ☐ Electrical
- ☐ Exhaust
- ☐ Other_________

INSTALL DETAILS

Installed by: ______________________________

Install time: (hrs)_________________________

Tools used: _______________________________

____

Torque Specs/Key Notes:_____________________

____

RESULTS:

Performance Change: _______________________

Further Adjustments:________________________

MODIFICATION ENTRY

Asset ID: __________
Owner: __________

ENTRY #:

Install Date: ________________________________

Mileage at Install: ________________________

PART INFORMATION

Part Name: ________________________________

Model #: ________________________________

Brand : ________________________________

Supplier: ________________________________

Website: ________________________________

Order #: ________________________________

COST BREAKDOWN

Parts Cost: $ ________________________________

Shipping: $ ________________________________

Tax: $ ________________________________

Labor: $ ________________________________

TOTAL INSTALL COST: $ ________________

Total Build Costs to Date: $ ____________

CATEGORY

- ☐ Engine
- ☐ Suspension
- ☐ Transmission
- ☐ Interior
- ☐ Exterior
- ☐ Wheels & Tires
- ☐ Electrical
- ☐ Exhaust
- ☐ Other________

INSTALL DETAILS

Installed by: ______________________________

Install time: (hrs)__________________________

Tools used: ________________________________

____

Torque Specs/Key Notes:______________________

____

RESULTS:

Performance Change: ________________________________

Further Adjustments:________________________________

MODIFICATION ENTRY

Asset ID: __________
Owner: __________

ENTRY #:

Install Date: _______________________________

 Mileage at Install: __________________________

PART INFORMATION

Part Name: _________________________________

Model #: ___________________________________

Brand : ____________________________________

Supplier: ___________________________________

Website: ___________________________________

Order #: ____________________________________

COST BREAKDOWN

Parts Cost: $ _______________________________

Shipping: $ _________________________________

Tax: $ _____________________________________

Labor: $ ___________________________________

TOTAL INSTALL COST: $ ______________________

Total Build Costs to Date: $ _________________

CATEGORY

☐ Engine

☐ Suspension

☐ Transmission

☐ Interior

☐ Exterior

☐ Wheels & Tires

☐ Electrical

☐ Exhaust

☐ Other__________

INSTALL DETAILS

Installed by: _______________________________

Install time: (hrs) __________________________

Tools used: ________________________________

____

Torque Specs/Key Notes: ____________________

____

RESULTS:

Performance Change: _______________________

Further Adjustments: ________________________

MODIFICATION ENTRY

Asset ID: _________

Owner: _________

ENTRY #:

Install Date: _______________________________

Mileage at Install: _____________________

PART INFORMATION

Part Name: _______________________________

Model #: _______________________________

Brand : _______________________________

Supplier: _______________________________

Website: _______________________________

Order #: _______________________________

COST BREAKDOWN

Parts Cost: $_______________________________

Shipping: $ _______________________________

Tax: $_______________________________

Labor: $ _______________________________

TOTAL INSTALL COST: $ _____________________

Total Build Costs to Date: $ ______________

CATEGORY

- ☐ Engine
- ☐ Suspension
- ☐ Transmission
- ☐ Interior
- ☐ Exterior
- ☐ Wheels & Tires
- ☐ Electrical
- ☐ Exhaust
- ☐ Other_________

INSTALL DETAILS

Installed by: _______________________________

Install time: (hrs)_______________________________

Tools used: _______________________________

____

Torque Specs/Key Notes: _______________________________

____

RESULTS:

Performance Change: _______________________________

Further Adjustments:_______________________________

MODIFICATION ENTRY

Asset ID: _________

Owner: _________

ENTRY #:

Install Date: _______________________

Mileage at Install: ___________________

PART INFORMATION

Part Name: _______________________

Model #: _______________________

Brand : _______________________

Supplier: _______________________

Website: _______________________

Order #: _______________________

COST BREAKDOWN

Parts Cost: $_______________________

Shipping: $ _______________________

Tax: $_______________________

Labor: $ _______________________

TOTAL INSTALL COST: $ _______________

Total Build Costs to Date: $ _____________

CATEGORY

- ☐ Engine
- ☐ Suspension
- ☐ Transmission
- ☐ Interior
- ☐ Exterior
- ☐ Wheels & Tires
- ☐ Electrical
- ☐ Exhaust
- ☐ Other_________

INSTALL DETAILS

Installed by: _______________________

Install time: (hrs)_______________________

Tools used: _______________________

____

Torque Specs/Key Notes:_______________________

____

RESULTS:

Performance Change: _______________________

Further Adjustments:_______________________

MODIFICATION ENTRY

Asset ID: _________

Owner: _________

ENTRY #:

Install Date: _______________________

Mileage at Install: _______________

PART INFORMATION

Part Name: ___________________________

Model #: _____________________________

Brand : ______________________________

Supplier: ____________________________

Website: _____________________________

Order #: _____________________________

COST BREAKDOWN

Parts Cost: $_________________________

Shipping: $ __________________________

Tax: $_______________________________

Labor: $ _____________________________

TOTAL INSTALL COST: $ ________________

Total Build Costs to Date: $ _________

CATEGORY

- ☐ Engine
- ☐ Suspension
- ☐ Transmission
- ☐ Interior
- ☐ Exterior
- ☐ Wheels & Tires
- ☐ Electrical
- ☐ Exhaust
- ☐ Other________

INSTALL DETAILS

Installed by: _______________________

Install time: (hrs)__________________

Tools used: ____

____

Torque Specs/Key Notes:______________________________________

____

RESULTS:

Performance Change: ____

Further Adjustments:____

MODIFICATION ENTRY

Asset ID: _________
Owner: _________

ENTRY #:

Install Date: _______________________________

 Mileage at Install: _____________________

PART INFORMATION

Part Name: _________________________________

Model #: ___________________________________

Brand : ____________________________________

Supplier: __________________________________

Website: ___________________________________

Order #: ___________________________________

COST BREAKDOWN

Parts Cost: $ ______________________________

Shipping: $ ________________________________

Tax: $_____________________________________

Labor: $ __________________________________

TOTAL INSTALL COST: $ _____________________

Total Build Costs to Date: $ _______________

CATEGORY

- ☐ Engine
- ☐ Suspension
- ☐ Transmission
- ☐ Interior
- ☐ Exterior
- ☐ Wheels & Tires
- ☐ Electrical
- ☐ Exhaust
- ☐ Other_________

INSTALL DETAILS

Installed by: _______________________________

Install time: (hrs)__________________________

Tools used: _________________________________

____

Torque Specs/Key Notes:______________________

____

RESULTS:

Performance Change: _________________________

Further Adjustments:_________________________

MODIFICATION ENTRY

Asset ID: _________
Owner: _________

ENTRY #:

Install Date: _______________________

 Mileage at Install: _________________

PART INFORMATION

Part Name: _______________________

Model #: _________________________

Brand : __________________________

Supplier: ________________________

Website: _________________________

Order #: _________________________

COST BREAKDOWN

Parts Cost: $_____________________________

Shipping: $ ______________________________

Tax: $ ___________________________________

Labor: $ _________________________________

TOTAL INSTALL COST: $ ___________________

Total Build Costs to Date: $ _____________

CATEGORY

- ☐ Engine
- ☐ Suspension
- ☐ Transmission
- ☐ Interior
- ☐ Exterior
- ☐ Wheels & Tires
- ☐ Electrical
- ☐ Exhaust
- ☐ Other_________

INSTALL DETAILS

Installed by: _____________________

Install time: (hrs)_______________________

Tools used: ____

____

Torque Specs/Key Notes:_______________________________________

____

RESULTS:

Performance Change: ____

Further Adjustments:____

MODIFICATION ENTRY

Asset ID: __________
Owner: __________

ENTRY #:

Install Date: _______________________________

 Mileage at Install: _______________________

PART INFORMATION

Part Name: _______________________________

Model #: _________________________________

Brand : __________________________________

Supplier: ________________________________

Website: _________________________________

Order #: _________________________________

COST BREAKDOWN

Parts Cost: $ _____________________________

Shipping: $ _______________________________

Tax: $ ____________________________________

Labor: $ __________________________________

TOTAL INSTALL COST: $ ____________________

Total Build Costs to Date: $ ______________

CATEGORY

- ☐ Engine
- ☐ Suspension
- ☐ Transmission
- ☐ Interior
- ☐ Exterior
- ☐ Wheels & Tires
- ☐ Electrical
- ☐ Exhaust
- ☐ Other__________

INSTALL DETAILS

Installed by: ____________________________

Install time: (hrs) ______________________

Tools used: _______________________________

____

Torque Specs/Key Notes: __________________

____

RESULTS:

Performance Change: _____________________

Further Adjustments: _____________________

MODIFICATION ENTRY

Asset ID: __________
Owner: __________

ENTRY #:

Install Date: _______________________________

 Mileage at Install: ___________________

PART INFORMATION

Part Name: _______________________________

Model #: _________________________________

Brand : __________________________________

Supplier: ________________________________

Website: _________________________________

Order #: _________________________________

COST BREAKDOWN

Parts Cost: $_____________________________

Shipping: $ ______________________________

Tax: $____________________________________

Labor: $ _________________________________

TOTAL INSTALL COST: $ ____________________

Total Build Costs to Date: $ _____________

CATEGORY

☐ Engine

☐ Suspension

☐ Transmission

☐ Interior

☐ Exterior

☐ Wheels & Tires

☐ Electrical

☐ Exhaust

☐ Other_________

INSTALL DETAILS

Installed by: _____________________________

Install time: (hrs)_______________________

Tools used: _______________________________

____

Torque Specs/Key Notes:____________________

____

RESULTS:

Performance Change: ______________________

Further Adjustments:_______________________

MODIFICATION ENTRY

Asset ID: _________
Owner: _________

ENTRY #:

Install Date: _______________________________

 Mileage at Install: ____________________

PART INFORMATION

Part Name: _______________________________

Model #: _________________________________

Brand : __________________________________

Supplier: ________________________________

Website: _________________________________

Order #: _________________________________

COST BREAKDOWN

Parts Cost: $______________________________

Shipping: $ ______________________________

Tax: $____________________________________

Labor: $ _________________________________

TOTAL INSTALL COST: $ ___________________

Total Build Costs to Date: $ _____________

CATEGORY

- ☐ Engine
- ☐ Suspension
- ☐ Transmission
- ☐ Interior
- ☐ Exterior
- ☐ Wheels & Tires
- ☐ Electrical
- ☐ Exhaust
- ☐ Other_________

INSTALL DETAILS

Installed by: ______________________________

Install time: (hrs) _________________________

Tools used: _______________________________

____

Torque Specs/Key Notes: ___________________

____

RESULTS:

Performance Change: ______________________

Further Adjustments:_______________________

MODIFICATION ENTRY

ENTRY #:

Install Date: ______________________________

 Mileage at Install: ____________________

PART INFORMATION

Part Name: ________________________________

Model #: __________________________________

Brand : ___________________________________

Supplier: __________________________________

Website: __________________________________

Order #: __________________________________

COST BREAKDOWN

Parts Cost: $ _____________________________

Shipping: $ _______________________________

Tax: $ ____________________________________

Labor: $ __________________________________

TOTAL INSTALL COST: $ _______________

Total Build Costs to Date: $ ____________

CATEGORY

- ☐ Engine
- ☐ Suspension
- ☐ Transmission
- ☐ Interior
- ☐ Exterior
- ☐ Wheels & Tires
- ☐ Electrical
- ☐ Exhaust
- ☐ Other________

INSTALL DETAILS

Installed by: ______________________________

Install time: (hrs)_________________________

Tools used: ________________________________

____

Torque Specs/Key Notes:_____________________

____

RESULTS:

Performance Change: _______________________

Further Adjustments:________________________

MODIFICATION ENTRY

Asset ID: _________

Owner: __________

ENTRY #:

Install Date: _______________________________

 Mileage at Install: ___________________

PART INFORMATION

Part Name: ______________________________

Model #: ________________________________

Brand : _________________________________

Supplier: ________________________________

Website: ________________________________

Order #: ________________________________

COST BREAKDOWN

Parts Cost: $_____________________________

Shipping: $ ______________________________

Tax: $___________________________________

Labor: $ _________________________________

TOTAL INSTALL COST: $ ___________________

Total Build Costs to Date: $ _______________

CATEGORY

☐ Engine

☐ Suspension

☐ Transmission

☐ Interior

☐ Exterior

☐ Wheels & Tires

☐ Electrical

☐ Exhaust

☐ Other_________

INSTALL DETAILS

Installed by: ______________________________

Install time: (hrs)___________________________

Tools used: ____

____

Torque Specs/Key Notes:____

____

RESULTS:

Performance Change: ____

Further Adjustments:____

MODIFICATION ENTRY

Asset ID: _________
Owner: _________

ENTRY #:

Install Date: _______________________________

 Mileage at Install: _____________________

PART INFORMATION

Part Name: _______________________________

Model #: _________________________________

Brand : __________________________________

Supplier: ________________________________

Website: _________________________________

Order #: _________________________________

COST BREAKDOWN

Parts Cost: $ _______________________________

Shipping: $ _________________________________

Tax: $ _____________________________________

Labor: $ ___________________________________

TOTAL INSTALL COST: $ ________________________

Total Build Costs to Date: $ _________________

CATEGORY

- ☐ Engine
- ☐ Suspension
- ☐ Transmission
- ☐ Interior
- ☐ Exterior
- ☐ Wheels & Tires
- ☐ Electrical
- ☐ Exhaust
- ☐ Other_________

INSTALL DETAILS

Installed by: _______________________________

Install time: (hrs) _________________________

Tools used: ____

____

Torque Specs/Key Notes: ____

____

RESULTS:

Performance Change: ____

Further Adjustments: ____

MODIFICATION ENTRY

Asset ID: _________

Owner: _________

ENTRY #:

Install Date: _______________________________

Mileage at Install: ____________________

PART INFORMATION

Part Name: _______________________________

Model #: _________________________________

Brand : __________________________________

Supplier: ________________________________

Website: _________________________________

Order #: _________________________________

COST BREAKDOWN

Parts Cost: $ _____________________________

Shipping: $ _______________________________

Tax: $ ___________________________________

Labor: $ _________________________________

TOTAL INSTALL COST: $ ____________________

Total Build Costs to Date: $ _____________

CATEGORY

- ☐ Engine
- ☐ Suspension
- ☐ Transmission
- ☐ Interior
- ☐ Exterior
- ☐ Wheels & Tires
- ☐ Electrical
- ☐ Exhaust
- ☐ Other_________

INSTALL DETAILS

Installed by: _______________________

Install time: (hrs) _________________

Tools used: ____

____

Torque Specs/Key Notes: ____

____

RESULTS:

Performance Change: ____

Further Adjustments: ____

MODIFICATION ENTRY

Asset ID: ________

Owner: ________

ENTRY #:

Install Date: _________________________

Mileage at Install: _________________

PART INFORMATION

Part Name: ___________________________

Model #: ____________________________

Brand : _____________________________

Supplier: ___________________________

Website: ____________________________

Order #: ____________________________

COST BREAKDOWN

Parts Cost: $ _________________________

Shipping: $ _________________________

Tax: $ _____________________________

Labor: $ ___________________________

TOTAL INSTALL COST: $ ________________

Total Build Costs to Date: $ ____________

CATEGORY

- ☐ Engine
- ☐ Suspension
- ☐ Transmission
- ☐ Interior
- ☐ Exterior
- ☐ Wheels & Tires
- ☐ Electrical
- ☐ Exhaust
- ☐ Other________

INSTALL DETAILS

Installed by: ________________________

Install time: (hrs)_____________________

Tools used: ____

Torque Specs/Key Notes: ____

RESULTS:

Performance Change: ____

Further Adjustments:____

MODIFICATION ENTRY

Asset ID: _________
Owner: _________

ENTRY #:

Install Date: _______________________

 Mileage at Install: _______________

PART INFORMATION

Part Name: _______________________

Model #: _______________________

Brand : _______________________

Supplier: _______________________

Website: _______________________

Order #: _______________________

COST BREAKDOWN

Parts Cost: $_______________________

Shipping: $_______________________

Tax: $_______________________

Labor: $_______________________

TOTAL INSTALL COST: $_______________

Total Build Costs to Date: $_____________

CATEGORY

- ☐ Engine
- ☐ Suspension
- ☐ Transmission
- ☐ Interior
- ☐ Exterior
- ☐ Wheels & Tires
- ☐ Electrical
- ☐ Exhaust
- ☐ Other_________

INSTALL DETAILS

Installed by: _______________________

Install time: (hrs)_______________________

Tools used: _______________________

____

Torque Specs/Key Notes:_______________________

____

RESULTS:

Performance Change: _______________________

Further Adjustments:_______________________

MODIFICATION ENTRY

Asset ID: ________

Owner: ________

ENTRY #:

Install Date: ___________________________

Mileage at Install: ___________________

PART INFORMATION

Part Name: ___________________________

Model #: ____________________________

Brand : _____________________________

Supplier: ____________________________

Website: ____________________________

Order #: ____________________________

COST BREAKDOWN

Parts Cost: $_________________________

Shipping: $ _________________________

Tax: $______________________________

Labor: $ ___________________________

TOTAL INSTALL COST: $ ________________

Total Build Costs to Date: $ _____________

CATEGORY

- ☐ Engine
- ☐ Suspension
- ☐ Transmission
- ☐ Interior
- ☐ Exterior
- ☐ Wheels & Tires
- ☐ Electrical
- ☐ Exhaust
- ☐ Other________

INSTALL DETAILS

Installed by: _________________________

Install time: (hrs)______________________

Tools used: ____

____

Torque Specs/Key Notes: ____

____

RESULTS:

Performance Change: ____

Further Adjustments:____

MODIFICATION ENTRY

Asset ID: _________
Owner: __________

ENTRY #:

Install Date: _________________________________

 Mileage at Install: ____________________________

PART INFORMATION

Part Name: _______________________________

Model #: _________________________________

Brand : __________________________________

Supplier: ________________________________

Website: _________________________________

Order #: _________________________________

COST BREAKDOWN

Parts Cost: $_____________________________________

Shipping: $ ______________________________________

Tax: $____

Labor: $ ____

TOTAL INSTALL COST: $ ____________________

Total Build Costs to Date: $ _______________

CATEGORY

- ☐ Engine
- ☐ Suspension
- ☐ Transmission
- ☐ Interior
- ☐ Exterior
- ☐ Wheels & Tires
- ☐ Electrical
- ☐ Exhaust
- ☐ Other_________

INSTALL DETAILS

Installed by: ______________________________

Install time: (hrs)__________________________

Tools used: ____

____

Torque Specs/Key Notes:____

____

RESULTS:

Performance Change: ____

Further Adjustments:____

MODIFICATION ENTRY

Asset ID: _________

Owner: _________

ENTRY #:

Install Date: _______________________________

 Mileage at Install: ____________________

PART INFORMATION

Part Name: _________________________________

Model #: ___________________________________

Brand : ____________________________________

Supplier: __________________________________

Website: ___________________________________

Order #: ___________________________________

COST BREAKDOWN

Parts Cost: $ ______________________________

Shipping: $ ________________________________

Tax: $ _____________________________________

Labor: $ ___________________________________

TOTAL INSTALL COST: $ ______________________

Total Build Costs to Date: $ ______________

CATEGORY

- ☐ Engine
- ☐ Suspension
- ☐ Transmission
- ☐ Interior
- ☐ Exterior
- ☐ Wheels & Tires
- ☐ Electrical
- ☐ Exhaust
- ☐ Other_________

INSTALL DETAILS

Installed by: ______________________________

Install time: (hrs)_________________________

Tools used: ________________________________

____

Torque Specs/Key Notes:_____________________

____

RESULTS:

Performance Change: _______________________

Further Adjustments:________________________

MODIFICATION ENTRY

Asset ID: _________

Owner: _________

ENTRY #:

Install Date: _______________________

Mileage at Install: _________________

PART INFORMATION

Part Name: _______________________

Model #: _________________________

Brand : __________________________

Supplier: ________________________

Website: _________________________

Order #: _________________________

COST BREAKDOWN

Parts Cost: $ ____________________

Shipping: $ _____________________

Tax: $ __________________________

Labor: $ ________________________

TOTAL INSTALL COST: $ ____________

Total Build Costs to Date: $ __________

CATEGORY

- ☐ Engine
- ☐ Suspension
- ☐ Transmission
- ☐ Interior
- ☐ Exterior
- ☐ Wheels & Tires
- ☐ Electrical
- ☐ Exhaust
- ☐ Other_________

INSTALL DETAILS

Installed by: ____________________

Install time: (hrs) _______________

Tools used: ____

____

Torque Specs/Key Notes: ___________________________________

____

RESULTS:

Performance Change: _______________________________________

Further Adjustments: _______________________________________

MODIFICATION ENTRY

Asset ID: _________

Owner: _________

ENTRY #:

Install Date: _______________________

 Mileage at Install: ________________

PART INFORMATION

Part Name: ___________________________

Model #: ___________________________

Brand : ___________________________

Supplier: ___________________________

Website: ___________________________

Order #: ___________________________

COST BREAKDOWN

Parts Cost: $___________________________

Shipping: $ ___________________________

Tax: $___________________________

Labor: $ ___________________________

TOTAL INSTALL COST: $ ___________________

Total Build Costs to Date: $ ______________

CATEGORY

- ☐ Engine
- ☐ Suspension
- ☐ Transmission
- ☐ Interior
- ☐ Exterior
- ☐ Wheels & Tires
- ☐ Electrical
- ☐ Exhaust
- ☐ Other_________

INSTALL DETAILS

Installed by: ___________________________

Install time: (hrs)___________________________

Tools used: ____

____

Torque Specs/Key Notes:____

____

RESULTS:

Performance Change: ____

Further Adjustments:____

MODIFICATION ENTRY

Asset ID: _________

Owner: _________

ENTRY #:

Install Date: _______________________

Mileage at Install: _______________

PART INFORMATION

Part Name: ___________________

Model #: ______________________

Brand : _______________________

Supplier: _____________________

Website: ______________________

Order #: ______________________

COST BREAKDOWN

Parts Cost: $ _________________________

Shipping: $ __________________________

Tax: $ _______________________________

Labor: $ _____________________________

TOTAL INSTALL COST: $ _______________

Total Build Costs to Date: $ ____________

CATEGORY

- ☐ Engine
- ☐ Suspension
- ☐ Transmission
- ☐ Interior
- ☐ Exterior
- ☐ Wheels & Tires
- ☐ Electrical
- ☐ Exhaust
- ☐ Other_________

INSTALL DETAILS

Installed by: ____________________

Install time: (hrs)_______________

Tools used: ____

____

Torque Specs/Key Notes:_______________________________________

____

RESULTS:

Performance Change: ____

Further Adjustments:____

MODIFICATION ENTRY

Asset ID: __________
Owner: __________

ENTRY #:

Install Date: _______________________

 Mileage at Install: _________________

PART INFORMATION

Part Name: _______________________

Model #: _______________________

Brand : _______________________

Supplier: _______________________

Website: _______________________

Order #: _______________________

COST BREAKDOWN

Parts Cost: $ _______________________

Shipping: $ _______________________

Tax: $ _______________________

Labor: $ _______________________

TOTAL INSTALL COST: $ _______________

Total Build Costs to Date: $ _____________

CATEGORY

- ☐ Engine
- ☐ Suspension
- ☐ Transmission
- ☐ Interior
- ☐ Exterior
- ☐ Wheels & Tires
- ☐ Electrical
- ☐ Exhaust
- ☐ Other_________

INSTALL DETAILS

Installed by: _______________________

Install time: (hrs)_______________________

Tools used: ____

____

Torque Specs/Key Notes: ____

____

RESULTS:

Performance Change: _____________________________________

Further Adjustments:____

MODIFICATION ENTRY

Asset ID: ________

Owner: ________

ENTRY #:

Install Date: _______________________________

 Mileage at Install: _________________________

PART INFORMATION

Part Name: _________________________

Model #: ___________________________

Brand : ____________________________

Supplier: __________________________

Website: ___________________________

Order #: ___________________________

COST BREAKDOWN

Parts Cost: $_________________________________

Shipping: $ _________________________________

Tax: $______________________________________

Labor: $ ___________________________________

TOTAL INSTALL COST: $ ______________________

Total Build Costs to Date: $ ________________

CATEGORY

- ☐ Engine
- ☐ Suspension
- ☐ Transmission
- ☐ Interior
- ☐ Exterior
- ☐ Wheels & Tires
- ☐ Electrical
- ☐ Exhaust
- ☐ Other________

INSTALL DETAILS

Installed by: _______________________

Install time: (hrs)__________________

Tools used: ____

____

Torque Specs/Key Notes:____

____

RESULTS:

Performance Change: ____

Further Adjustments:____

MODIFICATION ENTRY

ENTRY #:

Install Date: _______________________

 Mileage at Install: _______________

PART INFORMATION

Part Name: _____________________

Model #: _______________________

Brand : ________________________

Supplier: ______________________

Website: _______________________

Order #: _______________________

COST BREAKDOWN

Parts Cost: $_____________________

Shipping: $ _____________________

Tax: $__________________________

Labor: $ _______________________

TOTAL INSTALL COST: $ ____________

Total Build Costs to Date: $ __________

CATEGORY

- ☐ Engine
- ☐ Suspension
- ☐ Transmission
- ☐ Interior
- ☐ Exterior
- ☐ Wheels & Tires
- ☐ Electrical
- ☐ Exhaust
- ☐ Other________

INSTALL DETAILS

Installed by: ___________________

Install time: (hrs)________________

Tools used: ____

____

Torque Specs/Key Notes:_______________________________

____

RESULTS:

Performance Change: _________________________________

Further Adjustments:_________________________________

MODIFICATION ENTRY

Asset ID: _________

Owner: _________

ENTRY #:

Install Date: _______________________________

 Mileage at Install: _____________________

PART INFORMATION

Part Name: _______________________________

Model #: _________________________________

Brand : __________________________________

Supplier: ________________________________

Website: _________________________________

Order #: _________________________________

COST BREAKDOWN

Parts Cost: $_______________________________

Shipping: $ ________________________________

Tax: $____________________________________

Labor: $ __________________________________

TOTAL INSTALL COST: $ _______________________

Total Build Costs to Date: $ _________________

CATEGORY

- ☐ Engine
- ☐ Suspension
- ☐ Transmission
- ☐ Interior
- ☐ Exterior
- ☐ Wheels & Tires
- ☐ Electrical
- ☐ Exhaust
- ☐ Other_________

INSTALL DETAILS

Installed by: _______________________________

Install time: (hrs)___________________________

Tools used: _________________________________

____

Torque Specs/Key Notes: _____________________

____

RESULTS:

Performance Change: ________________________

Further Adjustments:_________________________

MODIFICATION ENTRY

Asset ID: ________

Owner: ________

ENTRY #:

Install Date: _______________________

 Mileage at Install: _________________

PART INFORMATION

Part Name: _______________________

Model #: _________________________

Brand : __________________________

Supplier: ________________________

Website: _________________________

Order #: _________________________

COST BREAKDOWN

Parts Cost: $ _____________________

Shipping: $ ______________________

Tax: $ __________________________

Labor: $ ________________________

TOTAL INSTALL COST: $ ____________

Total Build Costs to Date: $ __________

CATEGORY

- [ ] Engine
- [ ] Suspension
- [ ] Transmission
- [ ] Interior
- [ ] Exterior
- [ ] Wheels & Tires
- [ ] Electrical
- [ ] Exhaust
- [ ] Other________

INSTALL DETAILS

Installed by: ____________________

Install time: (hrs)_______________

Tools used: ____

____

Torque Specs/Key Notes:_________________________________

____

RESULTS:

Performance Change: ___________________________________

Further Adjustments:____________________________________

MODIFICATION ENTRY

Asset ID: ________

Owner: ________

ENTRY #:

Install Date: ________________________

Mileage at Install: ________________

PART INFORMATION

Part Name: ____________________

Model #: ____________________

Brand : ____________________

Supplier: ____________________

Website: ____________________

Order #: ____________________

COST BREAKDOWN

Parts Cost: $ ____________________

Shipping: $ ____________________

Tax: $ ____________________

Labor: $ ____________________

TOTAL INSTALL COST: $ ____________

Total Build Costs to Date: $ __________

CATEGORY

- ☐ Engine
- ☐ Suspension
- ☐ Transmission
- ☐ Interior
- ☐ Exterior
- ☐ Wheels & Tires
- ☐ Electrical
- ☐ Exhaust
- ☐ Other________

INSTALL DETAILS

Installed by: ____________________

Install time: (hrs) ________________

Tools used: ____________________

____

Torque Specs/Key Notes: ____________

____

RESULTS:

Performance Change: ________________

Further Adjustments: ________________

MODIFICATION ENTRY

Asset ID: _________

Owner: _________

ENTRY #:

Install Date: _______________________

 Mileage at Install: _______________________

PART INFORMATION

Part Name: _______________________

Model #: _______________________

Brand : _______________________

Supplier: _______________________

Website: _______________________

Order #: _______________________

COST BREAKDOWN

Parts Cost: $_______________________

Shipping: $ _______________________

Tax: $_______________________

Labor: $ _______________________

TOTAL INSTALL COST: $ _______________

Total Build Costs to Date: $ _____________

CATEGORY

- ☐ Engine
- ☐ Suspension
- ☐ Transmission
- ☐ Interior
- ☐ Exterior
- ☐ Wheels & Tires
- ☐ Electrical
- ☐ Exhaust
- ☐ Other_________

INSTALL DETAILS

Installed by: _______________________

Install time: (hrs)_______________________

Tools used: _______________________

____

Torque Specs/Key Notes: _______________________

____

RESULTS:

Performance Change: _______________________

Further Adjustments:_______________________

MODIFICATION ENTRY

Asset ID: _________
Owner: _________

ENTRY #:

Install Date: _________________________

 Mileage at Install: _______________________

PART INFORMATION

Part Name: _______________________________

Model #: _________________________________

Brand : __________________________________

Supplier: ________________________________

Website: _________________________________

Order #: _________________________________

COST BREAKDOWN

Parts Cost: $ ____________________________

Shipping: $ ______________________________

Tax: $ ___________________________________

Labor: $ _________________________________

TOTAL INSTALL COST: $ ____________________

Total Build Costs to Date: $ _____________

CATEGORY

☐ Engine

☐ Suspension

☐ Transmission

☐ Interior

☐ Exterior

☐ Wheels & Tires

☐ Electrical

☐ Exhaust

☐ Other_________

INSTALL DETAILS

Installed by: ____________________________

Install time: (hrs)______________________

Tools used: ______________________________

____

Torque Specs/Key Notes: __________________

____

RESULTS:

Performance Change: _____________________

Further Adjustments:_____________________

MODIFICATION ENTRY

ENTRY #:

Install Date: _________________________________

 Mileage at Install: ___________________________

PART INFORMATION

Part Name: _____________________________

Model #: ________________________________

Brand : _________________________________

Supplier: _______________________________

Website: _______________________________

Order #: ________________________________

COST BREAKDOWN

Parts Cost: $____________________________

Shipping: $ _____________________________

Tax: $__________________________________

Labor: $ _______________________________

TOTAL INSTALL COST: $ ___________________

Total Build Costs to Date: $ _______________

CATEGORY

- ☐ Engine
- ☐ Suspension
- ☐ Transmission
- ☐ Interior
- ☐ Exterior
- ☐ Wheels & Tires
- ☐ Electrical
- ☐ Exhaust
- ☐ Other_________

INSTALL DETAILS

Installed by: ___________________________

Install time: (hrs)_______________________

Tools used: ____

____

Torque Specs/Key Notes:____

____

RESULTS:

Performance Change: ____

Further Adjustments:____

MODIFICATION ENTRY

Asset ID: _________
Owner: _________

ENTRY #:

Install Date: _______________________

Mileage at Install: _______________

PART INFORMATION

Part Name: _______________________

Model #: _________________________

Brand : __________________________

Supplier: ________________________

Website: _________________________

Order #: _________________________

COST BREAKDOWN

Parts Cost: $_____________________

Shipping: $ ______________________

Tax: $___________________________

Labor: $ _________________________

TOTAL INSTALL COST: $ ____________

Total Build Costs to Date: $ ___________

CATEGORY

- ☐ Engine
- ☐ Suspension
- ☐ Transmission
- ☐ Interior
- ☐ Exterior
- ☐ Wheels & Tires
- ☐ Electrical
- ☐ Exhaust
- ☐ Other_________

INSTALL DETAILS

Installed by: _____________________

Install time: (hrs)_________________

Tools used: ____

Torque Specs/Key Notes:______________________________________

RESULTS:

Performance Change: _______________________________

Further Adjustments:_________________________________

MODIFICATION ENTRY

Asset ID: _________
Owner: _________

ENTRY #:

Install Date: _______________________

Mileage at Install: _______________

PART INFORMATION

Part Name: _______________________

Model #: _______________________

Brand : _______________________

Supplier: _______________________

Website: _______________________

Order #: _______________________

COST BREAKDOWN

Parts Cost: $_______________________

Shipping: $ _______________________

Tax: $_______________________

Labor: $ _______________________

TOTAL INSTALL COST: $ _______________

Total Build Costs to Date: $ _____________

CATEGORY

☐ Engine

☐ Suspension

☐ Transmission

☐ Interior

☐ Exterior

☐ Wheels & Tires

☐ Electrical

☐ Exhaust

☐ Other_________

INSTALL DETAILS

Installed by: _______________________

Install time: (hrs)_______________________

Tools used: _______________________

____

Torque Specs/Key Notes: _______________________

____

RESULTS:

Performance Change: _______________________

Further Adjustments:_______________________

MODIFICATION ENTRY

Asset ID: ________
Owner: ________

ENTRY #:

Install Date: _______________________

 Mileage at Install: ______________________

PART INFORMATION

Part Name: _______________________

Model #: _______________________

Brand : _______________________

Supplier: _______________________

Website: _______________________

Order #: _______________________

COST BREAKDOWN

Parts Cost: $_______________________

Shipping: $_______________________

Tax: $_______________________

Labor: $_______________________

TOTAL INSTALL COST: $______________

Total Build Costs to Date: $____________

CATEGORY

☐ Engine

☐ Suspension

☐ Transmission

☐ Interior

☐ Exterior

☐ Wheels & Tires

☐ Electrical

☐ Exhaust

☐ Other________

INSTALL DETAILS

Installed by: _______________________

Install time: (hrs)_______________________

Tools used: _______________________

____

Torque Specs/Key Notes:_______________________

____

RESULTS:

Performance Change: _______________________

Further Adjustments:_______________________

MODIFICATION ENTRY

Asset ID: _________
Owner: _________

ENTRY #:

Install Date: _______________________

 Mileage at Install: ________________

PART INFORMATION

Part Name: ____________________

Model #: ______________________

Brand : _______________________

Supplier: _____________________

Website: ______________________

Order #: ______________________

COST BREAKDOWN

Parts Cost: $ __________________

Shipping: $ ___________________

Tax: $ _______________________

Labor: $ _____________________

TOTAL INSTALL COST: $ _________

Total Build Costs to Date: $ _______

CATEGORY

☐ Engine

☐ Suspension

☐ Transmission

☐ Interior

☐ Exterior

☐ Wheels & Tires

☐ Electrical

☐ Exhaust

☐ Other________

INSTALL DETAILS

Installed by: ________________

Install time: (hrs)_______________

Tools used: ____________________

____

Torque Specs/Key Notes:____________

____

RESULTS:

Performance Change: ______________

Further Adjustments:________________

MODIFICATION ENTRY

Asset ID: _________
Owner: _________

ENTRY #:

Install Date: _______________________

 Mileage at Install: _________________

PART INFORMATION

Part Name: _____________________

Model #: _______________________

Brand : _______________________

Supplier: ______________________

Website: _______________________

Order #: _______________________

COST BREAKDOWN

Parts Cost: $_____________________

Shipping: $ _____________________

Tax: $__________________________

Labor: $ _______________________

TOTAL INSTALL COST: $ ______________

Total Build Costs to Date: $ ____________

CATEGORY

☐ Engine

☐ Suspension

☐ Transmission

☐ Interior

☐ Exterior

☐ Wheels & Tires

☐ Electrical

☐ Exhaust

☐ Other_________

INSTALL DETAILS

Installed by: ___________________

Install time: (hrs)________________

Tools used: ____

____

Torque Specs/Key Notes:____________________________________

____

RESULTS:

Performance Change: _________________________________

Further Adjustments:_________________________________

MODIFICATION ENTRY

Asset ID: _________

Owner: _________

ENTRY #:

Install Date: _______________________

Mileage at Install: _______________

PART INFORMATION

Part Name: _____________________________

Model #: _______________________________

Brand : ________________________________

Supplier: ______________________________

Website: _______________________________

Order #: _______________________________

COST BREAKDOWN

Parts Cost: $_____________________________

Shipping: $ _____________________________

Tax: $___________________________________

Labor: $ ________________________________

TOTAL INSTALL COST: $ ___________________

Total Build Costs to Date: $ ____________

CATEGORY

- ☐ Engine
- ☐ Suspension
- ☐ Transmission
- ☐ Interior
- ☐ Exterior
- ☐ Wheels & Tires
- ☐ Electrical
- ☐ Exhaust
- ☐ Other_________

INSTALL DETAILS

Installed by: _______________________

Install time: (hrs)_________________________

Tools used: ____

____

Torque Specs/Key Notes:________________________________

____

RESULTS:

Performance Change: ___________________________________

Further Adjustments:___________________________________

MODIFICATION ENTRY

Asset ID: ___________
Owner: ___________

ENTRY #:

Install Date: _______________________________

 Mileage at Install: _____________________

PART INFORMATION

Part Name: _______________________________

Model #: _________________________________

Brand : __________________________________

Supplier: ________________________________

Website: _________________________________

Order #: _________________________________

COST BREAKDOWN

Parts Cost: $ _____________________________

Shipping: $ _______________________________

Tax: $ ____________________________________

Labor: $ __________________________________

TOTAL INSTALL COST: $ _______________

Total Build Costs to Date: $ _____________

CATEGORY

- ☐ Engine
- ☐ Suspension
- ☐ Transmission
- ☐ Interior
- ☐ Exterior
- ☐ Wheels & Tires
- ☐ Electrical
- ☐ Exhaust
- ☐ Other_________

INSTALL DETAILS

Installed by: ______________________________

Install time: (hrs)_________________________

Tools used: ________________________________

____

Torque Specs/Key Notes:_____________________

____

RESULTS:

Performance Change: _______________________

Further Adjustments:________________________

MODIFICATION ENTRY

Asset ID: _________

Owner: _________

ENTRY #:

Install Date: _______________________

Mileage at Install: _______________

PART INFORMATION

Part Name: _______________________

Model #: _________________________

Brand : __________________________

Supplier: ________________________

Website: _________________________

Order #: _________________________

COST BREAKDOWN

Parts Cost: $_____________________

Shipping: $ ______________________

Tax: $ ___________________________

Labor: $ _________________________

TOTAL INSTALL COST: $ ____________

Total Build Costs to Date: $ __________

CATEGORY

☐ Engine

☐ Suspension

☐ Transmission

☐ Interior

☐ Exterior

☐ Wheels & Tires

☐ Electrical

☐ Exhaust

☐ Other_________

INSTALL DETAILS

Installed by: ____________________

Install time: (hrs)______________

Tools used: ______________________

____

Torque Specs/Key Notes:______________

____

RESULTS:

Performance Change: _________________

Further Adjustments:_________________

MODIFICATION ENTRY

Asset ID: _________

Owner: _________

ENTRY #:

Install Date: _______________________________

Mileage at Install: _______________________

PART INFORMATION

Part Name: _______________________________

Model #: _________________________________

Brand : __________________________________

Supplier: ________________________________

Website: _________________________________

Order #: _________________________________

COST BREAKDOWN

Parts Cost: $_____________________________

Shipping: $ ______________________________

Tax: $ ___________________________________

Labor: $ _________________________________

TOTAL INSTALL COST: $ ___________________

Total Build Costs to Date: $ _____________

CATEGORY

- [ ] Engine
- [ ] Suspension
- [ ] Transmission
- [ ] Interior
- [ ] Exterior
- [ ] Wheels & Tires
- [ ] Electrical
- [ ] Exhaust
- [ ] Other_________

INSTALL DETAILS

Installed by: _______________________________

Install time: (hrs) _________________________

Tools used: _________________________________

____

Torque Specs/Key Notes:______________________

____

RESULTS:

Performance Change: ________________________

Further Adjustments:_________________________

MODIFICATION ENTRY

Asset ID: _________
Owner: _________

ENTRY #:

Install Date: _______________________

 Mileage at Install: ________________

PART INFORMATION

Part Name: _____________________

Model #: _______________________

Brand : ________________________

Supplier: ______________________

Website: _______________________

Order #: _______________________

COST BREAKDOWN

Parts Cost: $_____________________

Shipping: $ _____________________

Tax: $ __________________________

Labor: $ ________________________

TOTAL INSTALL COST: $ _____________

Total Build Costs to Date: $ ___________

CATEGORY

- ☐ Engine
- ☐ Suspension
- ☐ Transmission
- ☐ Interior
- ☐ Exterior
- ☐ Wheels & Tires
- ☐ Electrical
- ☐ Exhaust
- ☐ Other_________

INSTALL DETAILS

Installed by: _____________________

Install time: (hrs)_________________

Tools used: _______________________

____

Torque Specs/Key Notes: ___________________

____

RESULTS:

Performance Change: ______________________

Further Adjustments:_______________________

MODIFICATION ENTRY

Asset ID: _________

Owner: _________

ENTRY #:

Install Date: _______________________

Mileage at Install: _______________

PART INFORMATION

Part Name: _____________________

Model #: _______________________

Brand : ________________________

Supplier: ______________________

Website: _______________________

Order #: _______________________

COST BREAKDOWN

Parts Cost: $ ___________________

Shipping: $ _____________________

Tax: $ __________________________

Labor: $ ________________________

TOTAL INSTALL COST: $ ___________

Total Build Costs to Date: $ ___________

CATEGORY

- ☐ Engine
- ☐ Suspension
- ☐ Transmission
- ☐ Interior
- ☐ Exterior
- ☐ Wheels & Tires
- ☐ Electrical
- ☐ Exhaust
- ☐ Other_________

INSTALL DETAILS

Installed by: ___________________

Install time: (hrs)________________

Tools used: _____________________

____

Torque Specs/Key Notes:_____________________

____

RESULTS:

Performance Change: _____________________

Further Adjustments:_____________________

MODIFICATION ENTRY

Asset ID: _________

Owner: _________

ENTRY #:

Install Date: _______________________

Mileage at Install: _________________

PART INFORMATION

Part Name: _______________________

Model #: _________________________

Brand : __________________________

Supplier: ________________________

Website: _________________________

Order #: _________________________

COST BREAKDOWN

Parts Cost: $ ______________________

Shipping: $ _______________________

Tax: $ ___________________________

Labor: $ _________________________

TOTAL INSTALL COST: $ ______________

Total Build Costs to Date: $ __________

CATEGORY

- ☐ Engine
- ☐ Suspension
- ☐ Transmission
- ☐ Interior
- ☐ Exterior
- ☐ Wheels & Tires
- ☐ Electrical
- ☐ Exhaust
- ☐ Other_________

INSTALL DETAILS

Installed by: _____________________

Install time: (hrs)________________

Tools used: ____

____

Torque Specs/Key Notes:_________________________________

____

RESULTS:

Performance Change: ____________________________________

Further Adjustments:_____________________________________

MODIFICATION ENTRY

Asset ID: _________
Owner: _________

ENTRY #:

Install Date: _________________________________

 Mileage at Install: _____________________

PART INFORMATION

Part Name: _______________________________

Model #: _________________________________

Brand : __________________________________

Supplier: ________________________________

Website: _________________________________

Order #: _________________________________

COST BREAKDOWN

Parts Cost: $ _______________________________

Shipping: $ _________________________________

Tax: $ ______________________________________

Labor: $ ____________________________________

TOTAL INSTALL COST: $ _______________________

Total Build Costs to Date: $ _______________

CATEGORY

- ☐ Engine
- ☐ Suspension
- ☐ Transmission
- ☐ Interior
- ☐ Exterior
- ☐ Wheels & Tires
- ☐ Electrical
- ☐ Exhaust
- ☐ Other_________

INSTALL DETAILS

Installed by: _______________________________

Install time: (hrs)_________________________

Tools used: _________________________________

____

Torque Specs/Key Notes: _____________________

____

RESULTS:

Performance Change: ________________________

Further Adjustments:_________________________

MAINTENANCE RECORD

Asset ID: _________

Owner: _________

Date	Mileage	Service Performed	Vendor	Cost	Next Due

Maintenance Notes:

____

____

MAINTENANCE RECORD

Asset ID: ________

Owner: ________

Date	Mileage	Service Performed	Vendor	Cost	Next Due

Maintenance Notes:

____

____

____

MAINTENANCE RECORD

Asset ID: ________

Owner: ________

Date	Mileage	Service Performed	Vendor	Cost	Next Due

Maintenance Notes:

____

____

____

MAINTENANCE RECORD

Asset ID: _________

Owner: _________

Date	Mileage	Service Performed	Vendor	Cost	Next Due

Maintenance Notes:

____

____

____

MAINTENANCE RECORD

Asset ID: ________

Owner: ________

Date	Mileage	Service Performed	Vendor	Cost	Next Due

Maintenance Notes:

MAINTENANCE RECORD

Asset ID: ________

Owner: ________

Date	Mileage	Service Performed	Vendor	Cost	Next Due

Maintenance Notes:

____

____

____

MAINTENANCE RECORD

Asset ID: _________

Owner: _________

Date	Mileage	Service Performed	Vendor	Cost	Next Due

Maintenance Notes:

____

____

____

MAINTENANCE RECORD

Asset ID: _________
Owner: _________

Date	Mileage	Service Performed	Vendor	Cost	Next Due

Maintenance Notes:

MAINTENANCE RECORD

Asset ID: _________

Owner: _________

Date	Mileage	Service Performed	Vendor	Cost	Next Due

Maintenance Notes:

____

____

MAINTENANCE RECORD

Asset ID: ________

Owner: ________

Date	Mileage	Service Performed	Vendor	Cost	Next Due

Maintenance Notes:

____

____

MAINTENANCE RECORD

Asset ID: _________
Owner: _________

Date	Mileage	Service Performed	Vendor	Cost	Next Due

Maintenance Notes:

MAINTENANCE RECORD

Asset ID: _________

Owner: _________

Date	Mileage	Service Performed	Vendor	Cost	Next Due

Maintenance Notes:

____

____

____

MAINTENANCE RECORD

Asset ID: _________

Owner: _________

Date	Mileage	Service Performed	Vendor	Cost	Next Due

Maintenance Notes:

____

____

MAINTENANCE RECORD

Asset ID: _________

Owner: _________

Date	Mileage	Service Performed	Vendor	Cost	Next Due

Maintenance Notes:

____

____

____

MAINTENANCE RECORD

Asset ID: _________
Owner: _________

Date	Mileage	Service Performed	Vendor	Cost	Next Due

Maintenance Notes:

MAINTENANCE RECORD

Asset ID: _________

Owner: _________

Date	Mileage	Service Performed	Vendor	Cost	Next Due

Maintenance Notes:

____

____

____

MAINTENANCE RECORD

Asset ID: ________

Owner: ________

Date	Mileage	Service Performed	Vendor	Cost	Next Due

Maintenance Notes:

____

____

____

MAINTENANCE RECORD

Asset ID: ________

Owner: ________

Date	Mileage	Service Performed	Vendor	Cost	Next Due

Maintenance Notes:

MAINTENANCE RECORD

Asset ID: _________
Owner: _________

Date	Mileage	Service Performed	Vendor	Cost	Next Due

Maintenance Notes:

____

____

MAINTENANCE RECORD

Asset ID: ________
Owner: ________

Date	Mileage	Service Performed	Vendor	Cost	Next Due

Maintenance Notes:

____

____

PERFORMANCE LOG - DYNO & BENCH TESTS

Asset ID: _________
Owner: _________

Date	Test	Equipment	Test Target	Result	Technician	Notes

PERFORMANCE LOG - DYNO & BENCH TESTS

Asset ID: ________
Owner: ________

Date	Test	Equipment	Test Target	Result	Technician	Notes

PERFORMANCE LOG - DYNO & BENCH TESTS

Asset ID: _________
Owner: _________

Date	Test	Equipment	Test Target	Result	Technician	Notes

PERFORMANCE LOG - DYNO & BENCH TESTS

Asset ID: _________

Owner: _________

Date	Test	Equipment	Test Target	Result	Technician	Notes

PERFORMANCE LOG - ROAD & TRACK TESTS

Asset ID: _________

Owner: _________

Test Date: _______________________   Engine Hours (optional): _____________

Location: _______________________   Fuel Type Used: ________________

Odometer Mileage: _______________   Weather(temp/humidity): _____________

TEST TYPE

☐ Dyno Pull   ☐ Track Day   ☐ Quarter Mile   ☐ Road Course

☐ Tuning Session   ☐ Rolling Dyno   ☐ Street Test   ☐ Other _________

CONFIGURATION AT TIME OF TEST

Engine configuration: ____

Boost level (if forced induction): _____________________________________

Fuel map: ____

Exhaust configuration: ____

Tire setup: ____

Suspension settings: ____

Changes since last test: ____

MEASURED RESULTS

If Dyno	**If Track/Drag**	**If Road Course**
Peak HP: _____________	Elapsed Time: ________	Lap Time: ____________
Peak Torque: __________	Trap Speed: _________	Track Name: __________
RPM at Peak HP: _______	Reaction Time: _______	Session Conditions: _______
RPM at Peak Torque: ____	60-ft Time: __________	____________________

DRIVER NOTES

Observations: ____

Issues noticed: ____

Tuning changes required: ____

Vibration/Heat/Traction notes: ____

PERFORMANCE LOG - ROAD & TRACK TESTS

Asset ID: _________
Owner: _________

Test Date: _____________________ Engine Hours (optional): _____________

Location: _____________________ Fuel Type Used: _____________________

Odometer Mileage: _______________ Weather(temp/humidity): _____________

TEST TYPE

☐ Dyno Pull   ☐ Track Day   ☐ Quarter Mile   ☐ Road Course

☐ Tuning Session   ☐ Rolling Dyno   ☐ Street Test   ☐ Other _______

CONFIGURATION AT TIME OF TEST

Engine configuration: _______________________________________

Boost level (if forced induction): ___________________________

Fuel map: ____

Exhaust configuration: ______________________________________

Tire setup: ____

Suspension settings: ____

Changes since last test: ____________________________________

MEASURED RESULTS

If Dyno	**If Track/Drag**	**If Road Course**
Peak HP: _____________	Elapsed Time:________	Lap Time: _____________
Peak Torque: __________	Trap Speed: _________	Track Name:____________
RPM at Peak HP: ________	Reaction Time: ________	Session Conditions: _______
RPM at Peak Torque:_____	60-ft Time: _________	_____________________

DRIVER NOTES

Observations: ____

Issues noticed: ____

Tuning changes required: ____________________________________

Vibration/Heat/Traction notes: ______________________________

PERFORMANCE LOG - ROAD & TRACK TESTS

Asset ID: _________
Owner: _________

Test Date: _________________________   Engine Hours (optional): _______________
Location: _________________________   Fuel Type Used: _________________________
Odometer Mileage: _______________   Weather(temp/humidity): _______________

TEST TYPE

☐ Dyno Pull   ☐ Track Day   ☐ Quarter Mile   ☐ Road Course

☐ Tuning Session   ☐ Rolling Dyno   ☐ Street Test   ☐ Other _______

CONFIGURATION AT TIME OF TEST

Engine configuration: ____
Boost level (if forced induction): ____
Fuel map: ____
Exhaust configuration: ____
Tire setup: ____
Suspension settings: ____
Changes since last test: ____

MEASURED RESULTS

If Dyno	**If Track/Drag**	**If Road Course**
Peak HP: _____________	Elapsed Time: _______	Lap Time: _____________
Peak Torque: __________	Trap Speed: ________	Track Name: __________
RPM at Peak HP: _______	Reaction Time: ______	Session Conditions: _______
RPM at Peak Torque: _____	60-ft Time: ________	_______________________

DRIVER NOTES

Observations: ____
Issues noticed: ____
Tuning changes required: ____
Vibration/Heat/Traction notes: ____

PERFORMANCE LOG - ROAD & TRACK TESTS

Asset ID: ___________

Owner: ___________

Test Date: ___________________________ Engine Hours (optional): ___________________

Location: _______________________ Fuel Type Used: _______________________

Odometer Mileage: _________________ Weather(temp/humidity): _______________

TEST TYPE

☐ Dyno Pull ☐ Track Day ☐ Quarter Mile ☐ Road Course

☐ Tuning Session ☐ Rolling Dyno ☐ Street Test ☐ Other ___________

CONFIGURATION AT TIME OF TEST

Engine configuration: ____

Boost level (if forced induction): ____

Fuel map: ____

Exhaust configuration: ____

Tire setup: ____

Suspension settings: ____

Changes since last test: ____

MEASURED RESULTS

If Dyno	**If Track/Drag**	**If Road Course**
Peak HP: ___________	Elapsed Time:_________	Lap Time: ___________
Peak Torque: _________	Trap Speed: _________	Track Name:___________
RPM at Peak HP: _______	Reaction Time:________	Session Conditions:________
RPM at Peak Torque: _____	60-ft Time: _________	___________________

DRIVER NOTES

Observations: ____

Issues noticed: ____

Tuning changes required: ____

Vibration/Heat/Traction notes: ____

PERFORMANCE LOG - ROAD & TRACK TESTS

Asset ID: _________
Owner: _________

Test Date: _____________________   Engine Hours (optional): _____________

Location: _____________________   Fuel Type Used: _______________

Odometer Mileage: ______________   Weather(temp/humidity): ___________

TEST TYPE

☐ Dyno Pull   ☐ Track Day   ☐ Quarter Mile   ☐ Road Course

☐ Tuning Session   ☐ Rolling Dyno   ☐ Street Test   ☐ Other _______

CONFIGURATION AT TIME OF TEST

Engine configuration: ____

Boost level (if forced induction): ______________________________

Fuel map: ____

Exhaust configuration: _______________________________________

Tire setup: ____

Suspension settings: ____

Changes since last test: _____________________________________

MEASURED RESULTS

If Dyno

Peak HP: _______________

Peak Torque: ____________

RPM at Peak HP: _________

RPM at Peak Torque: _____

If Track/Drag

Elapsed Time:_________

Trap Speed: __________

Reaction Time: _______

60-ft Time: __________

If Road Course

Lap Time: _______________

Track Name:_____________

Session Conditions: ______

____

DRIVER NOTES

Observations: ____

Issues noticed: ____

Tuning changes required: _____________________________________

Vibration/Heat/Traction notes: ________________________________

PERFORMANCE LOG - ROAD & TRACK TESTS

Asset ID: _________
Owner: _________

Test Date: _____________________   Engine Hours (optional): _____________
Location: _____________________   Fuel Type Used: _____________________
Odometer Mileage: _______________   Weather(temp/humidity): _____________

TEST TYPE

☐ Dyno Pull   ☐ Track Day   ☐ Quarter Mile   ☐ Road Course

☐ Tuning Session   ☐ Rolling Dyno   ☐ Street Test   ☐ Other _________

CONFIGURATION AT TIME OF TEST

Engine configuration: _________________________________
Boost level (if forced induction): _________________________
Fuel map: _________________________________
Exhaust configuration: _________________________________
Tire setup: _________________________________
Suspension settings: _________________________________
Changes since last test: _________________________________

MEASURED RESULTS

If Dyno	**If Track/Drag**	**If Road Course**
Peak HP: _____________	Elapsed Time:________	Lap Time: _____________
Peak Torque: __________	Trap Speed: _________	Track Name:____________
RPM at Peak HP: _______	Reaction Time:________	Session Conditions:_______
RPM at Peak Torque:____	60-ft Time: _________	_____________________

DRIVER NOTES

Observations: _________________________________
Issues noticed: _________________________________
Tuning changes required: _________________________________
Vibration/Heat/Traction notes: _________________________________

PERFORMANCE LOG - ROAD & TRACK TESTS

Asset ID: _________
Owner: _________

Test Date: _____________________
Location: _____________________
Odometer Mileage: _____________

Engine Hours (optional): _____________
Fuel Type Used: _____________
Weather(temp/humidity): _____________

TEST TYPE

☐ Dyno Pull   ☐ Track Day   ☐ Quarter Mile   ☐ Road Course

☐ Tuning Session   ☐ Rolling Dyno   ☐ Street Test   ☐ Other ________

CONFIGURATION AT TIME OF TEST

Engine configuration: _____________________________________
Boost level (if forced induction): ________________________________
Fuel map: ____
Exhaust configuration: ____________________________________
Tire setup: ____
Suspension settings: ______________________________________
Changes since last test: ___________________________________

MEASURED RESULTS

If Dyno	**If Track/Drag**	**If Road Course**
Peak HP: _____________	Elapsed Time:________	Lap Time: _____________
Peak Torque: __________	Trap Speed: _________	Track Name:____________
RPM at Peak HP: ________	Reaction Time: _______	Session Conditions: ______
RPM at Peak Torque:_____	60-ft Time: __________	_____________________

DRIVER NOTES

Observations: ____
Issues noticed: _______________________________________
Tuning changes required: ______________________________
Vibration/Heat/Traction notes: ________________________

PERFORMANCE LOG - ROAD & TRACK TESTS

Asset ID: _________

Owner: _________

Test Date: _____________________ Engine Hours (optional): _____________

Location: _____________________ Fuel Type Used: _______________________

Odometer Mileage: ________________ Weather(temp/humidity): ______________

TEST TYPE

☐ Dyno Pull   ☐ Track Day   ☐ Quarter Mile   ☐ Road Course

☐ Tuning Session   ☐ Rolling Dyno   ☐ Street Test   ☐ Other ________

CONFIGURATION AT TIME OF TEST

Engine configuration: ____

Boost level (if forced induction): ______________________________

Fuel map: ____

Exhaust configuration: ____

Tire setup: ____

Suspension settings: ____

Changes since last test: ______________________________________

MEASURED RESULTS

If Dyno

Peak HP: _______________

Peak Torque: ___________

RPM at Peak HP: ________

RPM at Peak Torque: ____

If Track/Drag

Elapsed Time: ________

Trap Speed: _________

Reaction Time: ______

60-ft Time: _________

If Road Course

Lap Time: _______________

Track Name: _____________

Session Conditions: ______

____

DRIVER NOTES

Observations: ____

Issues noticed: ____

Tuning changes required: _________________________________

Vibration/Heat/Traction notes: ___________________________

SHOW, MEDIA, & PERFORMANCE MILESTONES

Asset ID: _________
Owner: _________

Date: ____

Event Name: ____

Location: ____

Type: ☐ Show   ☐ Track   ☐ Award   ☐ Media   ☐ Other

Result: ____

Notes: ____

Links: ____

Date: ____

Event Name: ____

Location: ____

Type: ☐ Show   ☐ Track   ☐ Award   ☐ Media   ☐ Other

Result: ____

Notes: ____

Links: ____

Date: ____

Event Name: ____

Location: ____

Type: ☐ Show   ☐ Track   ☐ Award   ☐ Media   ☐ Other

Result: ____

Notes: ____

Links: ____

SHOW, MEDIA, & PERFORMANCE MILESTONES

Asset ID: _________

Owner: _________

Date: ____

Event Name: ____

Location: ____

Type: ☐ Show   ☐ Track   ☐ Award   ☐ Media   ☐ Other

Result: ____

Notes: ____

Links: ____

Date: ____

Event Name: ____

Location: ____

Type: ☐ Show   ☐ Track   ☐ Award   ☐ Media   ☐ Other

Result: ____

Notes: ____

Links: ____

Date: ____

Event Name: ____

Location: ____

Type: ☐ Show   ☐ Track   ☐ Award   ☐ Media   ☐ Other

Result: ____

Notes: ____

Links: ____

SHOW, MEDIA, & PERFORMANCE MILESTONES

Asset ID: _________

Owner: _________

Date: ____

Event Name: ____

Location: ____

Type: ☐ Show   ☐ Track   ☐ Award   ☐ Media   ☐ Other

Result: ____

Notes: ____

Links: ____

Date: ____

Event Name: ____

Location: ____

Type: ☐ Show   ☐ Track   ☐ Award   ☐ Media   ☐ Other

Result: ____

Notes: ____

Links: ____

Date: ____

Event Name: ____

Location: ____

Type: ☐ Show   ☐ Track   ☐ Award   ☐ Media   ☐ Other

Result: ____

Notes: ____

Links: ____

SHOW, MEDIA, & PERFORMANCE MILESTONES

Asset ID: ________

Owner: ________

Date: ______________________________________

Event Name: ____________________________

Location: ______________________________

Type: ☐ Show ☐ Track ☐ Award ☐ Media ☐ Other

Result: ________________________________

Notes: _________________________________

Links: _________________________________

Date: ____________________________________

Event Name: ____________________________

Location: ______________________________

Type: ☐ Show ☐ Track ☐ Award ☐ Media ☐ Other

Result: ________________________________

Notes: _________________________________

Links: _________________________________

Date: ____________________________________

Event Name: ____________________________

Location: ______________________________

Type: ☐ Show ☐ Track ☐ Award ☐ Media ☐ Other

Result: ________________________________

Notes: _________________________________

Links: _________________________________

SHOW, MEDIA, & PERFORMANCE MILESTONES

Asset ID:________
Owner:________

Date: _______________________________

Event Name: _________________________

Location:____________________________

Type: ☐ Show   ☐ Track   ☐ Award   ☐ Media   ☐ Other

Result: _____________________________

Notes: ______________________________

Links: ______________________________

Date: _______________________________

Event Name: _________________________

Location:____________________________

Type: ☐ Show   ☐ Track   ☐ Award   ☐ Media   ☐ Other

Result: _____________________________

Notes: ______________________________

Links: ______________________________

Date: _______________________________

Event Name: _________________________

Location:____________________________

Type: ☐ Show   ☐ Track   ☐ Award   ☐ Media   ☐ Other

Result: _____________________________

Notes: ______________________________

Links: ______________________________

INVESTMENT & VALUATION SUMMARY

INVESTMENT SUMMARY BY CATEGORY

Category	Parts Investment	Labor Investment	Total
Engine	$	$	$
Transmission	$	$	$
Suspension	$	$	$
Electrical	$	$	$
Interior	$	$	$
Paint & Body	$	$	$
Wheels & Tires	$	$	$
Other	$	$	$

Total Parts Investment: ____

Total Labor Investment: ____

Total Documented Build Investment:______________________________

Estimated Self-Performed Labor Value: ___________________________

Estimated Total Build Cost: _____________________________________

INVESTMENT & VALUATION SUMMARY

DECLARED VALUE STATEMENT

ACQUISITION BASELINE

Original Purchase Date: ————————————

Purchased From: ————————————

Original Purchase Price: ———————————

DOCUMENTED INVESTMENT

Total Parts Investment (from Modification Entries): ____________________

Total Professional Labor Investment: __________________________

Sub-total (Parts & Professional Labor): $ _______________________

ESTIMATED SELF-PERFORMED LABOR VALUE

Self-performed Labor Hours:_____hrs

Estimated Professional Equivalent Labor Rate: ____$/hr
Estimated Total Self-performed Labor Value: $ ____________________

TOTAL ESTIMATED REPLACEMENT COST

Original Purchase Price: ——————————————————————

+Total Parts Investment: ________________________________

+Professional Labor Investment: _________________________

+Estimated Self-performed Labor Value: _____________________

= Estimated Total Replacement Cost: $ ______________________

INVESTMENT & VALUATION SUMMARY

DECLARED VALUE STATEMENT

Declared Value:____

Effective Date:____

This document reflects documented build investment and estimated replacement cost. It is not a formal appraisal and does not constitute an insurance valuation.

INVESTMENT & VALUATION SUMMARY

MARKET COMPARABLES

Comparable #:____

Vehicle Description: ____

Source: ____

Sale Price: ____

Date Sold: ____

Link: ____

Notes on Similarity: ____

Comparable #:____

Vehicle Description: ____

Source: ____

Sale Price: ____

Date Sold: ____

Link: ____

Notes on Similarity: ____

Comparable #:____

Vehicle Description: ____

Source: ____

Sale Price: ____

Date Sold: ____

Link: ____

Notes on Similarity: ____

INVESTMENT & VALUATION SUMMARY

Asset ID:________

Owner:________

MARKET COMPARABLES

Comparable #:____

Vehicle Description: ____________________________________

Source: ____

Sale Price: ____

Date Sold: ____

Link: ____

Notes on Similarity: ___________________________________

Comparable #:____

Vehicle Description: ____________________________________

Source: ____

Sale Price: ____

Date Sold: ____

Link: ____

Notes on Similarity: ___________________________________

Comparable #:____

Vehicle Description: ____________________________________

Source: ____

Sale Price: ____

Date Sold: ____

Link: ____

Notes on Similarity: ___________________________________

INVESTMENT & VALUATION SUMMARY

MARKET COMPARABLES

Comparable #:____
Vehicle Description: ____
Source: ____
Sale Price: ____
Date Sold: ____
Link: ____
Notes on Similarity: ____

Comparable #:____
Vehicle Description: ____
Source: ____
Sale Price: ____
Date Sold: ____
Link: ____
Notes on Similarity: ____

Comparable #:____
Vehicle Description: ____
Source: ____
Sale Price: ____
Date Sold: ____
Link: ____
Notes on Similarity: ____

PARTS RESEARCH LOG

Asset ID: _________
Owner: _________

Component	Vendor	Quoted Price	Decision	Notes

PARTS RESEARCH LOG

Asset ID: _________
Owner: _________

Component	Vendor	Quoted Price	Decision	Notes

PARTS RESEARCH LOG

Asset ID: _________

Owner: _________

Component	Vendor	Quoted Price	Decision	Notes

PARTS RESEARCH LOG

Asset ID: ________
Owner: ________

Component	Vendor	Quoted Price	Decision	Notes

PARTS RESEARCH LOG

Asset ID: ________

Owner: ________

Component	Vendor	Quoted Price	Decision	Notes

ADDITIONAL NOTES

ADDITIONAL NOTES

ADDITIONAL NOTES

Asset ID: ________

Owner: ________

ADDITIONAL NOTES

Asset ID: _________
Owner: _________

ADDITIONAL NOTES

www.ingramcontent.com/pod-product-compliance
Lightning Source LLC
Chambersburg PA
CBHW040144110726
48005CB00018B/2646